Hooray for She, He, Ze, and They!

For Little Lindz; I wrote this for you
—L. A.

To all LGBTQ+ young people
—K. A.

SIMON & SCHUSTER BOOKS FOR YOUNG READERS
An imprint of Simon & Schuster Children's Publishing Division
1230 Avenue of the Americas, New York, New York 10020
Text © 2024 by Queer Kid Creative, LLC
Illustration © 2024 by Kip Alizadeh
Book design by Laurent Linn © 2024 by Simon & Schuster, Inc.
Simon & Schuster: Celebrating 100 Years of Publishing in 2024
For information about special discounts for bulk purchases, please contact Simon & Schuster Special Sales
at 1-866-506-1949 or business@simonandschuster.com.
The Simon & Schuster Speakers Bureau can bring authors to your live event. For more information or to book an event,
contact the Simon & Schuster Speakers Bureau at 1-866-248-3049 or visit our website at www.simonspeakers.com.
The text for this book was set in Filson Soft.
The illustrations for this book were rendered with 6B pencil linework, watercolor textures, and pastel textures,
which were scanned and colored digitally using Adobe Photoshop.
Manufactured in China
1023 SCP
First Edition
2 4 6 8 10 9 7 5 3 1
Library of Congress Cataloging-in-Publication Data
Names: Amer, Lindz, author. | Alizadeh, Kip, illustrator.
Title: Hooray for she, he, ze, and they! : what are your pronouns today? / Lindz Amer ; illustrated by Kate Alizadeh.
Description: First edition | New York : Simon & Schuster Books for Young Readers, [2024] | Audience: Ages 4–8 | Audience: Grades K–1 |
Summary: "A young informational storybook introducing the concept of pronouns and identifying one's pronouns to kids"—Provided by publisher.
Identifiers: LCCN 2022053287 (print) | LCCN 2022053288 (ebook) | ISBN 9781665931144 (hardcover) | ISBN 9781665931151 (ebook)
Subjects: LCSH: Gender identity—Juvenile literature.
Classification: LCC HQ18.552 .A55 2024 (print) | LCC HQ18.552 (ebook) | DDC 305.3—dc23/eng/20230407
LC record available at https://lccn.loc.gov/2022053287
LC ebook record available at https://lccn.loc.gov/2022053288

Hooray for She, He, Ze, and They!

What Are YOUR Pronouns Today?

Written by
Lindz Amer

Illustrated by
Kip Alizadeh

SIMON & SCHUSTER BOOKS FOR YOUNG READERS

New York   London   Toronto   Sydney   New Delhi

Hi, friend!

I'm Lindz, and my pronouns are they/them.
What are your pronouns today?
What's a pronoun, you ask?
Well, everyone has pronouns!

We use pronouns to tell people about our gender.
Gender is that tingly feeling inside that tells you who you
are and how you want to express yourself to the world.

You can express your gender in
LOTS of different ways!

Like through your clothes

or your hairstyle

or your **pronouns.**

There are different pronouns that help us express our gender.
There are hes and there are shes.

There are theys.
There are zes and hirs and faes and pers.

You can choose your own pronouns.
Use whichever feels right to you,

because the right pronouns feel
super-cool-totally-awesome-amazingly-wonderful,
just like YOU!

When someone uses your right pronouns, it feels like pulling on your favorite sweater that fits just right, or like a warm hug from your favorite person when you're lonely.

It's like when you get to sit in your favorite seat at lunch,

or when your cup of hot cocoa is just hot enough to sip on a cold day,

or when you find your best stuffed friend
after you thought they were lost forever.

It's like remembering
which toothbrush is yours,

or belting your favorite song
at the top of your lungs,

or when your parent makes your
favorite food for dinner.

It makes you wanna do cartwheels through the playground,

jump so high on your parents' bed that you can touch the ceiling,

and throw a dance party with all your friends!

My pronouns make me feel like ME.

So what pronouns do you use?

Do *he* and *him* feel as cozy as sleeping
under a million blankets?

he* him

Do she and her feel like smiling so much that your cheeks might fall off?

she her

Do they and them feel like you can jump so high, you can say "hello" to the moon and the stars?

Or maybe you want to use
something totally different.

Or maybe you don't know your
pronouns yet. That's okay too.

But whatever pronouns you choose,
they should make you feel like **YOU!**

Super-cool-totally-awesome-
amazingly-wonderful
YOU!

So what do you say? What are
your pronouns today?

Dear Grown-ups!

When I was a kid, I wish I'd had the language to talk about my gender. *She* and *her* never quite felt right, but *he* and *him* felt a whole lot worse. I was assigned female at birth, so I was *expected* to wear dresses and grow my hair long, but I really just wanted to run around in corduroy overalls and keep my hair short and shaggy. That was *gender euphoria* for me. That's the feeling I'm describing in this book! When I'm feeling gender euphoric, my outsides match my insides, and there are very few better feelings. It's the opposite of gender dysphoria, when your outsides don't match your insides, and it feels extremely uncomfortable. When I hear someone use the wrong pronouns for me, it feels like a million tiny pinpricks in my heart. That feeling overcame me in my adolescence after years of being misgendered and not having the language to challenge it. So I hope you can use this book to talk to the children in your lives about how and when they feel *gender euphoria*. They can use that new recognition to explore what pronouns they want to use and how they want to express and communicate their gender to the rest of the world! It's what I wish I had when I was their age.

Love, Lindz

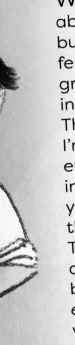

I was inspired to make the art for this book by all the beautiful people I know in the LGBTQ+ community. I wanted to show how incredible and euphoric it is when we can be ourselves, and when we celebrate other people being themselves too! I used lots of watercolor and pencil textures, as well as swirls and stars, to make this book as magical and full of possibility as I could.

—Kip